5 More of You!

Written by Darryl E. Green
and Mary Rose M. Green

Illustrated by Valerie Bouthyette

© 2013 Darryl E. Green and Mary Rose M. Green All rights reserved.
Five More of You
ISBN-13:978-0997500318
ISBN-10:099750031X

No part of this book may be reproduced, stored in a retrieval system, or transmitted by any means, electronic, mechanical, photocopying, recording, or otherwise, without written permission from the author.

Requests for speaking events, extra book copies or permissions should be addressed to greenspublications@gmail.com. Published by Greens' Publications, www.greenspublications.com.

Printed in the United States of America.

To our children, Allie and Tori, our parents, all of our siblings, our cousins and our nieces and nephews; your love, presence and many happy family moments were our inspiration for this book.

Before you were here, not too long ago,
Our life was all right but often seemed slow.
So we got some pets to make things upbeat.
But soon were beset by fur, paws and tweets.

We heard good advice, while seeing our vet.
He said, "Have some kids, ease up on the pets."

So soon we had one, and then we had two,
And we were just thrilled to have both of you.

Of course some things changed- our free time was less
Our small car was full, our house was a mess.
But those kinds of things did not bother us
You gave so much love and so little fuss.

So since life improved, because we had you
We thought, Why stop here? Why only have two?
We like being parents, it's working out fine,
And since that's the case, perhaps now's the time.

We weighed it all out and thought it all through,
But two kids plus one, meant more work to do.
More bottoms to clean, more diapers to toss,
More spit-up on shirts, more outfits to wash.
More feedings at night, to break up our sleep.
Less time for just us, less room in our Jeep.

We finally said, "We could do another.
A sister perhaps, or else a brother."

"And though life would change by growing our crew, all would be loved if we had more of you."

If three was okay, then what about four?
What would it be like, to add in two more?
More food to be made, more laundry to clean,
More kids in time out, who fought or got mean.

More things to be fixed, more pets on the couch, more fibs to address to make Dad a grouch.

"No problem!" We said. "Sure we could do four!
Because after all, four is only two more."

And though life would change by growing our crew,
all would be loved if we had more of you.

Raising four children would be really neat,
But raising five kids? A much bigger feat.
Five bellies to tickle, fifty toes to tweak,
Counting those piggies would take us all week.

Preparing for school would be quite a test,
In fact, I'm quite sure it'd be dreadful at best.
But five could be done. We could work it all out,
Since kids and family is what life is about.

And though life would change by growing our crew,
All would be loved if we had more of you.

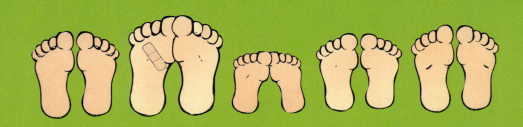

Most parents would say, "Five kids are ENOUGH!"
But no way, not us, we like this kid stuff.
Why stop at just five when you could have six?
Three boys and three girls, now that's a nice mix.
To bathe all those kids we might need a hand.
And no more cool Jeep; we'd trade for a van!

Yes, six would be hard, but we'd be just fine.
Others have six kids all of the time.

And though life would change by growing our crew,
All would be loved if we had more of you.

If six kids could be raised then seven could too.
Although some may say, "Yikes! Why won't six do?
Don't you value time? Don't you like to rest?
You should stop at six, that'd really be best."

But we'd make it work and do what we must,
Like trade in our van for a large school bus.

We know we'd be fine, with five more of you,
Although seven is more, so much more than two.

And though life would change by growing our crew,
All would be loved if we had more of you.

But then we said "Wait! Let's stop with this thought!
"It's hard enough with the two that we've got."
We'll focus on them and just wait and see,
Because after all, what will be will be."
And so here we are a family of four,
Quite happy for now and not adding more.

But if we should have, say,
FIFTEEN of you,
We'd figure things out
and more than make do.

Note to Parents and Educators:

We hope you enjoyed reading *Five More of You*. As you probably discovered, the story was written with many educational dimensions in mind. First, the theme of decision making is central to the story. The young Mom and Dad faced a very challenging (yet common) problem when they considered growing their family.

Second, *Five More of You* was written with a very mixed rhyming pattern and sequence that is not typically found in Children's' literature. Rhyming can be very useful in not only challenging reading aloud skills but in also helping to develop skills like reading cadence and pace.

Third, the wording used in the text to describe adding more children was purposefully made a little tricky to make the reader think carefully about the math.

Finally, some age-appropriate vocabulary is introduced for children in the K-3 range.

Reflection

Vocabulary

- See if you know what each of these words from the story means: advice, although, beset, crew, despite, feat, focus, improved, value, weighed.

Math

- There were many different pets in the story. How many did you see? What types?

- If the Mom and Dad decided to have 12 more kids, how many would they have all together?

- If they had decided to have 7 kids all together, how many could have been boys and how many could have been girls?"

- How many kids do you think could have fit on the family school bus?

Art

- See if you can draw a baby carriage that would hold 7 kids. Try to make it realistic, since Mom and Dad would need to use it if they had 7 children.

Values

- Why did the Mom and Dad care about what would happen if they had more children?

- Have you ever faced a decision where you had to think very carefully on what to do or what could happen? What did you do and why?

Meet the Authors

In addition to *Five More of you*, Darryl and Mary Rose Green are the authors of *Jake and the Buggy Melee* and *The Rules*, all illustrated by renowned children's book illustrator, Valerie Bouthyette. They have also authored works of fiction, non-fiction, poetry and academic research.

Mary Rose and Darryl are the proud parents of two amazing daughters and enjoy hiking, the arts, nature, their pets and trying to stay fit.

To learn more, or to schedule Mary Rose or Darryl for an event or presentation, please visit: www.greenspublications.com

Made in the USA
Lexington, KY
13 September 2018